Animals of Rivers, Lakes, and Ponds

By Sandra Donovan

Steadwell Books

Raintree Steck-Vaughn Publishers

A Harcourt Company

Austin · New York

www.raintreesteckvaughn.com

Published by Raintree Steck-Vaughn Publishers, an imprint of Steck-Vaughn Company.

Library of Congress Cataloging-in-Publication Data
Donovan, Sandra.
    Animals of rivers, lakes, and ponds / Sandra Donovan.
        p. cm. -- (Animals of the biomes)
    Summary: Describes the physical characteristics, behavior, adaptations, and life cycle of four animals that live in rivers, lakes, and ponds: the great blue heron, giant water bug, raccoon, and snapping turtle.
    Includes bibliographical references.
    ISBN 0-7398-5690-1 (hc); 0-7398-6411-4 (pbk).
        1. Freshwater animals--Juvenile literature. [1. Freshwater animals.]
    I. Title. II. Series.

QL141 .D65 2002
591.76--dc21   2002069713

Printed and bound in the United States of America
1 2 3 4 5 6 7 8 9 10 WZ 05 04 03 02 01

Produced by Compass Books

Photo Acknowledgments
Digital Stock, cover, 1, 24, 27, 28, 42, 45; Comstock, 40; South Dakota Tourism, 4, 8, 11, 14; Len Messineo, 13; Gerald and Cynthia Merker, 16; Dave Spier, 18; Gary Meszaros, 20; David Wrobel, 22; Thomas Kitchin, 30; Kitchin and Hurst, 32; John Gerlach, 35, 44; Joe McDonald, 36, 45; Dale Jackson, 39.

Content Consultant
Gary Wellborn
Department of Zoology, University of Oklahoma

This book supports the National Science Standards.

Contents

Animals such as this great blue heron live in and near rivers, lakes, and ponds.

Animals in Rivers, Lakes, and Ponds

Two-thirds of Earth is water. Only 3 percent of this is rivers, lakes, and ponds. Most rivers, lakes, and ponds are freshwater. This means there is little or no salt in the water.

Rivers, lakes, and ponds are one of Earth's biomes. A biome is a large region, or area, made of communities. A community is a group of certain plants and animals that live in the same place. Other biomes include forests, oceans, and deserts.

The water in rivers, lakes, and ponds is either moving or still. Ponds and lakes are still water. They do not move, or flow, into any body of water. Rivers are bodies of moving water. Many rivers flow into lakes or down from mountains.

Labels on map:
Arctic Ocean
North America
Great Lakes
Mississippi River
Pacific Ocean
Atlantic Ocean
Europe
Caspian Sea
Asia
Yangtze River
Africa
Nile River
Amazon River
South America
Indian Ocean
Australia
Antarctica
N W E S

This map shows some of Earth's major rivers and lakes.

What Lives in Rivers, Lakes, and Ponds?

All living things need water to live. Some animals spend most or all of their time in the water, and some come to the water only to drink. Many different plants and animals have adapted to live in rivers, lakes, and ponds.

Plants in and near rivers, lakes, and ponds need sunlight to live and grow. Most of the plants that live in the water live close to the surface.

Animals that like very warm climates may live near a tropical river, lake, or pond. Climate is the usual weather of an area over a period of time. It includes the amount of rain or snow, the temperature, and the wind. Tropical areas are where the climate is usually warm and wet. Other animals may like very cold climates. They may live near or even underneath a frozen river, lake, or pond. When a lake is frozen on top, there is still water under the ice. When this water contains enough oxygen, fish and other animals can still live there.

In the following chapters, you will learn about four different kinds of animals that live in rivers, lakes, and ponds. Birds called great blue herons spend much of their day standing in water. Giant water bugs scoot across the surface of water. **Mammals** called raccoons are active around water at night. Reptiles called snapping turtles live in the water and can break bones with their strong bite.

A great blue heron's long neck allows it to strike quickly at fish under the surface of the water.

The Great Blue Heron

The great blue heron is a bird. Birds are warm-blooded animals that have a backbone, wings, feathers, and a beak. Warm-blooded animals have a body temperature that stays more or less the same, no matter what the temperature of the air or water around them. Most birds can fly, but not all animals that fly are birds. Great blue herons can fly.

The scientific name for great blue herons is ardea herodias (ARE-dee-ah her-ODE-ih-as). These words actually mean "heron heron." Ardea means "heron" in Latin. Herodios means "heron" in Greek. Nicknames for the great blue heron are big cranky, blue crane, gray crane, and long john.

Great blue herons are bluish-gray. They have a black stripe above each eye that reaches to the back of the neck and turns into a plume of feathers. A plume is a showy grouping of long feathers. Great blue herons have a long, large yellow beak. Their legs are long and gray with reddish thighs.

Herons are usually between 39 and 52 inches (99–132 cm) long. Their wings can measure up to 6 feet (183 cm) across. They usually weigh between 5 and 8 pounds (2.3–3.6 kg).

Where Do Great Blue Herons Live?

All great blue herons live in North America, in the countries of the United States, Canada, and Mexico. They live as far north and west as Alaska, as far south as Mexico, and as far east as Nova Scotia.

Great blue herons can survive in both saltwater and freshwater habitats. A habitat is a place where an animal or plant usually lives. In saltwater, great blue herons live along ocean coasts. In freshwater, they are found in rivers, lakes, and ponds.

Unlike most birds, great blue herons allow their long legs to hang in the air behind them while flying.

Great blue herons are able to move about easily by flying. When they fly, their wings flap up and down very slowly and their long necks curl up. They can fly as fast as 29 miles (54 km) per hour.

How Have Great Blue Herons Adapted to Live in Rivers, Lakes, and Ponds?

Great blue herons are specially built to live in rivers, lakes, and ponds. They can stand still in shallow water for very long periods of time. This allows them to hunt for fish without being noticed. When a great blue heron is hunting, only its eyes and head move.

A great blue heron's bill is made for fishing. It comes to a sharp point that the bird can use to stab a fish. Their bills are very light and strong.

A heron is also able to hide from its enemies. Its color is very similar to the color of the water it lives in. This makes it difficult to see, especially when it is standing still. Herons also build their nests in trees high off the ground. Enemies that cannot climb or fly cannot reach them while they are sleeping. The nests also protect the heron's eggs and its young from predators.

What a Great Blue Heron Eats

Great blue herons eat mostly fish. They are carnivores. A **carnivore** is an animal that eats

This great blue heron will throw its neck back and swallow the captured fish whole.

only meat. Great blue herons also eat frogs, snakes, insects, mice, and small birds. They hunt for fish in two ways. One way is called "standing." This just means that they stand still in a shallow pool of water. They wait very quietly until a fish comes by, then stab it or grab it with their bills and eat it in one gulp.

▲ Because these herons are nesting in a tree, they will be safe from predators that cannot climb.

Walking Slowly

The other way that these birds hunt for fish is called "walking slowly." This is really closer to swimming than walking. The herons swim very slowly and stretch out their neck along the top of the water. When a fish swims by, they snatch it up quickly.

A Great Blue Heron's Life Cycle

When they are looking for a mate, male great blue herons make loud squawks. They have low, scratchy voices. After they mate, the female bird lays eggs in a nest. Both the male and female take care of the eggs until they hatch.

More than two out of three baby great blue herons do not live past their first birthday. This is because many predators feed on herons. A predator is an animal that hunts other animals for food. Predators of young great blue herons include other birds, snakes, and raccoons. They will eat both young herons and heron eggs.

Great blue herons are social birds. This means they live close together in colonies. A **colony** is a group of the same kind of animal that live together. Great blue herons usually build nests in treetops nearby water. Sometimes they also build nests on cliffs, on rock ledges, or on the ground near water.

If they survive their first year, great blue herons are likely to live for a long time. The oldest great blue heron on record lived to be more than 23 years old.

Of its three main body parts, the giant water bug's abdomen is largest.

The Giant Water Bug

Giant water bugs are a kind of insect. Insects are animals that have six legs and a body divided into three parts. The three parts of an insect's body are the head, **thorax**, and **abdomen**. The abdomen holds the stomach. The thorax is between the head and the abdomen. Most insects also have wings.

The scientific name for giant water bugs is abedus herberti (A-bih-dus her-BER-tee). Many people call them toe-biters. This is because they have a sharp front beak that they can use to stab. They sometimes stab people's toes as they walk through shallow water.

Most giant water bugs are about 1.5 inches (3.8 cm) long. Some grow up to 4 inches (10 cm).

> **This frontal view of a giant water bug shows its front legs, closed beak, eyes, and head.**

Giant water bugs are brown and flat and look like cockroaches. They have two long front legs and also two back legs covered with short hair. They have wings but hardly ever fly. They have a breathing tube that allows them to breathe while they are underwater.

Where Do Giant Water Bugs Live?

Giant water bugs are found in many places in the world. Mostly they live in North America, South Africa, and India. They also live in China.

The natural habitat of the giant water bug is freshwater. They usually live in slow-moving streams and rivers. They do not live in fast-moving rivers because they would be swept away by the current. Then they would not be able to find food.

How Have Giant Water Bugs Adapted to Live in Rivers, Lakes, and Ponds?

Several adaptations help giant water bugs live in rivers, lakes, and ponds. Because of their breathing tubes, they can be in the water all the time and still get the air they need to live.

Sometimes the rivers or streams where giant water bugs live dry up for part of the year. This is when they use their wings. When they cannot find enough food where they are living, they fly a short distance to find more water.

This giant water bug is eating prey that it has captured and injected with poison.

Playing Dead

One survival method that a giant water bug uses is to play dead. It can lie still without moving for a long time. When it does this, it looks like a small leaf. This helps keep its prey from knowing it is there. Prey are the animals that a predator eats. Playing dead also helps a water bug hide from predators.

What a Giant Water Bug Eats

Giant water bugs spend most of their time in the water looking for food to eat. They are an important part of the food chain in rivers and streams. The food chain is the normal cycle of living things eating other living things in nature. Giant water bugs are carnivores that eat other small insects, tadpoles, and small fish. These animals are their prey. In turn, giant water bugs are the prey for other large insects, fish, snakes, mice, and other animals.

Giant water bugs catch their prey with their two front legs. They are able to grab with these legs. Then they inject a poison into their prey to kill it before they eat it.

This newborn giant water bug is crawling on its father's back, where its egg is still attached.

A Giant Water Bug's Life Cycle

When giant water bugs are ready to mate, the female looks for a male. She lays eggs on the male's back. She may lay about 150 eggs on her mate's back. The male makes a kind of glue that makes the eggs stick to his back.

Then the male carries these eggs around for about three weeks until they hatch. He keeps them from getting moldy. Objects get moldy when too much water causes a growth to form. The male prevents mold by making sure they get enough air. Once the eggs hatch, the glue on the male's back dries up and the egg shells fall off.

Young giant water bugs are yellow when they first hatch from the egg. Within a few hours, they are brown like their parents. They turn from yellow to brown as their exoskeleton hardens.

As soon as they hatch, they are on their own. They usually stay close to the top of the water for a few weeks. This makes it easier for them to breathe. After 8 to 10 weeks, they are adults.

Raccoons' black eye masks have caused some people to nickname them "bandits."

The Raccoon

Raccoons are mammals. A mammal is a warm-blooded animal with a backbone. Mammals give birth to live young that they feed with milk from their own bodies. The scientific name for raccoons is rocyon (ROCK-yoon). A very common nickname for raccoon is coons.

Raccoons are covered with hair. This helps to keep them warm. Their hair is reddish-brown on top. On their undersides, it is black or gray. Their tails usually have four to six black or brown rings around them.

Raccoons have a very unusual face. It is pointy and it looks like a black mask outlined in white.

Raccoons have a bushy tail. They have two short legs in back and two in front. On their front legs they have claws that can grab things.

Raccoons are about 18 to 30 inches (46–76 cm) long. That does not include their bushy tail. The tail alone can be 8 to 12 inches (20–30 cm) long.

Where Do Raccoons Live?

Raccoons live all over North America. They are found as far north as southern Canada and as far south as South America. Most raccoons live in the United States.

The natural habitat for raccoons is wooded areas near lakes and streams. They like to live near the water, but they do not usually live near fast-moving rivers. Sometimes they live near the ocean, in marshes. A **marsh** is an area of soft, wet land. Many raccoons also live in towns and cities. Scientists say that raccoons will live wherever they can find food.

Raccoons make their homes in big holes called dens. They have their dens in hollow trees and logs, caves, and holes in the ground.

A raccoon uses its long fingers and hands to open, hold, and grab things, and to fight and climb.

Raccoons are excellent climbers. They can go to the far limbs of trees to escape predators such as dogs and cats.

Finding a Home

Sometimes raccoons even live in storm drains. One thing they do not do is make their own holes. Instead, they like to find places where there are already holes big enough for a den.

How Have Raccoons Adapted to Live in Rivers, Lakes, and Ponds?

Raccoons have adapted to live near almost any kind of water. They can eat almost anything and can make their dens almost anywhere. This makes it easier for them to move to a new habitat if they need to. Sometimes animals have to move to a new habitat because the old one is **polluted** or has dried up.

Raccoons can even adapt to living near people. They are not afraid of people and often find dens close to people's homes. They have been known to make their homes inside chimneys, in basements, in attics, between walls, and under patios. They can find food in the garbage that people throw away.

Raccoons are also good fighters. If attacked, they can use their strong paws like hands. If they are near water, they can even drown an enemy they are fighting. When they live near people in cities and towns, raccoons can fight off domestic cats and dogs.

> Raccoons will eat most anything they find, and have been know to steal food from campers.

What a Raccoon Eats

Raccoons are **nocturnal** animals. This means they sleep during the day and are active at night. They spend many of their night hours looking for food. They eat almost everything they can find. They are **omnivores**, meaning they eat both plants and other animals.

Raccoons eat nuts, fruits, berries, small fish, eggs, worms, and even small animals like mice. They also like to eat garbage left by people. Campers know that raccoons might even try to steal their food.

A Raccoon's Life Cycle

Raccoons usually mate in February or March. About two and a half months later, female raccoons give birth to their young. Young raccoons are called cubs. A female raccoon can have between two and seven cubs at once. The cubs are covered with hair. Cubs cannot see for almost 20 days after they are born.

Young raccoons live with their mothers until they are about 6 months old. At first the mother carries them with her mouth, holding them by their necks, like cats do. The mothers feed their young with mother's milk. This is called nursing. Young raccoons nurse until they are 6 weeks old.

Raccoons are not fully grown until they are 2 years old. Raccoons live from 6 to 12 years. Adult raccoons are **solitary** animals. This means they like to live alone, instead of in groups.

This snapping turtle has opened its mouth to look threatening. It does this to scare away people and predators.

The Snapping Turtle

Snapping turtles are reptiles. A reptile is an animal with a backbone that breathes air. Reptiles will either crawl on their bellies or on very short legs. Reptiles are cold-blooded. Cold-blooded means that an animal's body temperature stays about the same as the air or water around it.

The scientific name for snapping turtle is chelydra serpentina (che-LYE-dra SER-pen-teen-a). They are called snapping turtles because they have such strong jaws. They are very aggressive and will snap their jaws at almost anything.

Snapping turtles have brown shells with three ridges running along them. It is easier to see these ridges on young snapping turtles than it is on older turtles. Their skin can be gray, brown, yellow, tan, or black. Sometimes they have white dots on their skin.

Snapping turtles have four legs with heavy scales and webbed feet. Webbed means the toes are joined together with skin. This makes it easier to swim. They also have a long neck and large head. Their tail is sometimes as long as the rest of their body. It has three rows of high scales on it.

Snapping turtles can grow as large as 18 or 19 inches (46–48 cm) long. They can weigh up to 86 pounds (939 kg). Male snapping turtles are usually larger than females.

Where Do Snapping Turtles Live?

Snapping turtles live in North America. They are found as far north as southern Canada and throughout the United States, Central America, and South America.

Most people incorrectly think that snapping turtles are slow. Once on land, they can move quite quickly.

Freshwater is the natural habitat of snapping turtles. They usually live in shallow ponds or streams. Sometimes they live near the edges of deeper lakes and rivers. Snapping turtles prefer to live in slow-moving water with muddy bottoms. This is because they like to bury themselves in the mud.

> Snapping turtles spend most of their time at the bottom of most lakes and ponds where there are few or no predators.

Hibernation

In most of the United States and in Canada, snapping turtles **hibernate** in the mud in the winter. To hibernate means to remain in a very deep, sleeplike state during cold weather. In warmer climates, snapping turtles remain active all year round.

How Have Snapping Turtles Adapted to Live in Rivers, Lakes, and Ponds?

Snapping turtles are well adapted to live in rivers, lakes, and ponds. They can hold their breath for a long time. They must come to the surface of the water to breathe, but they do not have to do so very often. They can stay under the water, where it is easier to hunt and they are safer from enemies.

A kind of snapping turtle called the alligator snapper uses its tongue to trick the fish that it eats. The tongue looks like a worm. The turtle sits with its mouth open at the bottom of a river, lake, or pond. When fish see the tongue, they try to eat it, thinking it is a worm. Then the turtle snaps its mouth shut and eats the fish.

Snapping turtles can also use their strong, sharp jaws to fight any animals that try to attack them. Or they can pull their head and legs into their thick, strong shell to hide from enemies.

What a Snapping Turtle Eats

Snapping turtles are nocturnal. During the day, they usually bury themselves in the mud or sand at the bottom of a stream or pond. Here they sleep and may wait for prey to swim by. Snapping turtles eat fish, frogs, and other small animals that live in the water. They swallow them whole.

At night, snapping turtles are more active and will go out of the water to hunt for food. Because snapping turtles eat plants as well as animals and insects, they are considered omnivores.

A Snapping Turtle's Life Cycle

Snapping turtles usually mate in April or May. After mating, the female finds a place on land to dig a hole to lay her eggs in. The eggs keep warm in the hole until they hatch. It takes from 75 to 95 days for the eggs to hatch. Newborn snapping turtles are about one inch (27 mm) long.

After about three weeks, young snapping turtles leave the hole and crawl under a leaf or other object on the ground to hide. Then they

These snapping turtles have just hatched, and are an easy lunch to hungry predators that may spot them.

begin to crawl toward the nearest water. This can take many days. When they finally reach the water, they take a long drink. Then when they are full, they find another place to hide.

After about five years a snapping turtle is considered an adult. They normally live from 30 to 40 years.

When their habitats disappear, animals like this yellow-crowned night heron produce fewer young and their populations decline.

What Will Happen to Animals in Rivers, Lakes, and Ponds?

Rivers, lakes, and ponds provide a special habitat for the animals that live in and near them. Many plants and animals could not live anywhere else but in the freshwater of the river, lake, and pond biome.

Rivers, lakes, and ponds have often become polluted with garbage and other things thrown out or left behind by people. Chemicals from factories, farms, and manufacturing plants are another major cause of pollution. Plants and animals can die when freshwater becomes polluted.

Many rivers, lakes, and ponds are drained so that people can build on the land. The animals and plants that used to live there have to find new places to live.

Freshwater habitats like this pond are disappearing, and animals such as this great blue heron have fewer places to find food.

How are River, Lake, and Pond Animals Doing?

Great blue herons are losing their freshwater habitat. Many of the trees that they nest in are being cut down by people who want to make things with the wood. This is called logging.

Logging is a big business in many places where great blue herons live. One of the places where there is a lot of logging is the northwest United States, in the states of Washington and Oregon.

Unlike many other kinds of animals, giant water bugs and raccoons are not in danger of dying out. They are able to adapt to almost any kind of water habitat. Because they can adapt so well, raccoons are actually growing in number.

The biggest enemy of the snapping turtle is humans. Many humans hunt snapping turtles all over the United States and Canada. They try to trap them. This is because many people like to eat snapping turtles. People also hunt them to sell them to zoos. There are many snapping turtles living in zoos all across the United States.

Rivers, lakes, and ponds disappear every year. People are responsible for most of these disappearances. Because there is only a limited supply of freshwater, people need to think about how to use it wisely. None of us can live without it.

Quick Facts

Many animals that live in rivers, lakes, and ponds spend time both in the water and on the land near the water. This turtle is crawling onto land to do something, such as sun itself or lay eggs, that it cannot do in the water.

Giant water bugs and smaller water bugs common in many North American rivers, lakes, and ponds look and behave alike. The major difference among them is size.

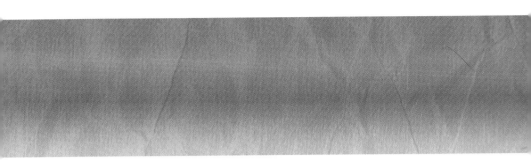

Raccoons can be dangerous to people because they may carry rabies, a disease that can be fatal and can spread to people if they are bitten.

Many animals, like this snapping turtle, can live in freshwater but not in saltwater. Only a few kinds of animals can live in both freshwater and saltwater.

Glossary

abdomen (AB-duh-min)—the part of an insect's body that holds its stomach

carnivore (KAHR-nuh-vor)—an animal that eats other animals

colony (KAH-lohn-ee)—a group of the same kind of animals that live together

hibernate (HEYE-bur-nayt)—to spend the winter in a deep, sleeplike state

mammal (MAM-uhl)—a warm-blooded animal that has a backbone, breathes air, and gives birth to live young

marsh (MARSH)—an area of soft, wet land

nocturnal (nok-TUR-nuhl)—active at night

omnivore (AHM-nee-vohr)—an animal that eats both plants and animals

polluted (Puh-LOO-ted)—dirtied with waste from human activity

solitary (SOL-ih-tar-ee)—an animal that likes to live alone

thorax (THO-raks)—the part of an insect's body between its abdomen and its head.

Addresses and Internet Sites

Kids for Saving Earth
P.O. Box 96090
Minneapolis, MN 55442

National Wildlife Federation
1400 16th Street, NW
Washington, D.C. 20036

Environment Canada
4905 Dufferin Street
Downsview, Ontario
M3H 5T4

Water Pollution
www.ala.org/ICONN/
KCFAQ/waterpollution.
htm

How can kids help?
www.rbff-
education.org/cgi-
bin/search/rbff.cgi?ID
=980812335

Books to Read

Braun, Eric and Donovan, Sandra. *Rivers, Lakes, and Ponds.* Austin, TX: Steck-Vaughn, 2001.

Braun, Eric and Donovan, Sandra. *Scientists of Rivers, Lakes, and Ponds.* Austin, TX: Steck-Vaughn, 2001.

Index